Get It Together

How to Organize Everything in Your Life

D0837351

-You!

Get It Together

How to Organize
Everything in
Your Life

By Julia Marsden

SCHOLASTIC INC.
New York Toronto London Auckland Sydney
Mexico City New Delhi Hong Kong

No part of this publication may be reproduced in whole or in part,
or stored in a retrieval system, or transmitted in any form or by any means,
electronic, mechanical, photocopying, recording, or otherwise, without
written permission of the publisher. For information regarding permission,
write to Petersen Publishing Company, L.L.C., 6420 Wilshire Boulevard,
Los Angeles, CA 90048-5515.

ISBN 0-439-13547-8

Copyright © 1999 by Petersen Publishing Co.

All About You! is a trademark of Petersen Publishing Company, L.L.C.,
and is used with permission. All rights reserved. Published by
Scholastic Inc., 555 Broadway, New York, NY 10012, under license from
Petersen Publishing Company. SCHOLASTIC and associated logos are
trademarks and/or registered trademarks of Scholastic Inc.

12 11 10 9 8 7 6 5 4 3   0 1 2 3 4 5/0

Printed in the U.S.A.   01

First Scholastic trade paperback printing, April 2000

I wish to thank my family and friends for their encouragement, understanding, and humor. Also, my thanks to Sara Fiedelholtz and Scholastic editors Susan Bishansky and Susan DerKazarian for their expert editorial advice and assistance.

Table of Contents

Section One: Priorities

Section Two: Places

Section Three: Planning

Introduction

Operation Organization

Does a typical day for you start with ransacking your room in search of last night's homework and then practically tripping over your own shoelaces as you motor out the door to school? Well, there's a better way. Why not trade in your current crash-and-burn system for some instant organization? There are plenty of reasons why it pays to get organized, and it's easier than you might think to set up a system that'll let you sail through a stress-free day without a major meltdown. . . .

First off, you should get set with a strategy. What is it you're after? A room that doesn't look like it's been hit by a hurricane? A calendar that's not totally crammed? A social life in which your friends are still speaking to you (unlike that time you endured some serious silent treatment because you blew them off by forgetting to meet them at the mall)? This get-organized guide will get you on track by letting you choose the areas you want to focus on most. So prepare to streamline your life with the step-by-step strategies you'll find in the chapters ahead!

Still wondering what's in it for you?

How about . . .

⚙ More time to do the stuff you love most

⚙ A sense of more space in your room

⚙ A cooler and more coordinated wardrobe

⚙ Way less stress

⚙ And a much mellower daily routine

Sounds pretty good, huh?

Keep reading for tons of ideas, examples, tricks, and tips. And get set to get organized!

Chapter One

Reasons to Get Organized

Find yourself wondering where the time goes? Feel like every minute of your day is already action-packed and there's no way you can add anything else to your daily routine? Well, by rethinking how you use your time, you can take back some of that super-scarce commodity to do the things you really want to do.

If you're at all interested in getting your act together, there's something you should know: Ultimately, organization is all about freeing up more time for yourself. 'Cause when you're wasting time searching for your house key or redoing a homework assignment because you've misplaced it, you're taking up time that could be put to better use. Instead of viewing planning and prioritizing projects as annoyances, pull back and take a glance at the big picture. This is what you'll see: By managing your time (and your space) better, you'll be managing your life better, too. This chapter will start things off by helping you get a grip on the stuff that's most important to you. It will give you some strategies to set specific goals for yourself and offer some options for accomplishing them.

Ready to take that first step? To do that you'll have to figure out what matters most to you. The people, activities, and things that rank right up there at the top of your list of priorities should be on the receiving end of the majority of your time and energy. Are you prepared to prioritize? While what follows isn't likely to leave you laughing out loud like a David Letterman top ten list does, it is gonna be just the kind of fill-in-the-blanks exercise to get you going in the right direction. So fill in the ten slots on the next page with the stuff that strikes you as most important. Not quite sure where to begin?

Here are some possible top tens:

- ✸ Doing well in school.
- ✸ Getting in shape.
- ✸ Getting along with my family.
- ✸ Saving more money.
- ✸ Volunteering each week.
- ✸ Spending time with my friends.

OK, it's your turn:

My Personal Top Ten List of Priorities

1. Get good grades
2. Clean up better
3. Save a lot of money
4. work with my show animals more
5. listen better
6. _____
7. _____
8. _____
9. _____
10. _____

Easy enough, right? Now, here's where things get a little more involved. For each of the ten priorities you listed, create a four-step Formula for Success chart like this:

⭐ My Formula for Success ⭐	
What I Want to Do:	do my spelling homework in one night
One Way I'll Make It Happen:	stop watching T.V.
Another Way I'll Make It Happen:	Do it on the bus
Still Another Way I'll Make It Happen:	Do it during free time

On the next page is an example of what a completed chart might look like:

⚝ My Formula for Success ⚝

What I Want to Do:	*Improve my math grade.*
One Way I'll Make It Happen:	*Study an additional fifteen minutes each night.*
Another Way I'll Make It Happen:	*Take better notes in class.*
Still Another Way I'll Make It Happen:	*Look into meeting with a tutor once a week.*

So what do you accomplish by completing your Formula for Success charts? Plenty! By actually writing down your priorities, you end up reflecting on what matters most to you and where your energy should be directed. You also take some time to look at new ways of tackling the tasks at hand. If you start thinking that there's *nothing* you can do about your grades or there's no way you can get in shape in time for summer, just refer to your Formula for Success charts. You'll see that you've already made some major headway by creating a to-do list that will help you get where you wanna be. Plus, if you pull out one of these charts a few months from now, you'll be amazed by how much you've accomplished in areas of your life that probably initially struck you as overwhelming. This can be just the kind of catalyst you need to set even more goals for yourself!

As you fill in your Formula for Success charts, ask yourself an important question: Are the goals I'm setting realistic and achievable? While you may *really* want to buy a portable CD player, if your only income at the moment is from baby-sitting once every couple of months, that's something that may not be all that realistic unless you take some major action. Or if you want to get ready for the upcoming soccer season, trying to master every skill in a week is just not gonna happen.

Once you've got your Formula for Success charts filled out in a way that seems realistic and workable, you can start to make some of those dreams come true. Need a little more inspiration? Read on for some additional advice.

To make your new way of thinking really work:

1. You should stick with goals that are specific. It's much more effective to write down "I will study an hour more every day," instead of "I'll study more." If you list something in a vague and undefined way, you're much less likely to accomplish the task. Why? The task is still in the planning stages. You haven't spelled it out yet!

2. You should commit to making things happen. Half the battle of setting goals and seeing results is remembering that success starts in your head. As in, if your mind-set says you can get the job done, you *will* get the job done. If you approach any new task with the outlook that you're not really capable of pulling it off, your defeatist attitude may very well do you in.

3. You'll need to give yourself a deadline. If you want to improve your grade in social studies class, just telling yourself that probably isn't enough to get results. Make a pact with yourself that includes a calendar. Why not tell yourself, "I'm going to bring up my grade by next week when the teacher is giving us a quiz on the chapter we just read." By being specific and plugging in to what it is you want, you can pinpoint when you'll be seeing some results.

4. **You should share your what-you-want-to-do list with someone who supports you.** When investigators arrive at the scene of a crime, one of the first things they try to determine is whether or not there were any witnesses. People who can back up what happened. Folks who can say what they saw or heard. If you let a friend or relative know what it is you want to achieve, you have an eyewitness who can remind you of what you said and help you avoid committing the crime of not accomplishing what you set out to do!

5. **You should hang out with people who will support your efforts.** So there's that friend of yours who's always upbeat and positive, never discouraging. Then there's your bud who's big on bad news and gloom and doom. Who's the one you'll turn to when you're trying to get your life in order? Friend #1? Good guess. Why even bother with a bad-news bearer? The last thing you need is a naysayer who tries to talk you out of going after a goal before your feet have even left the starting blocks. Stick with the friends who will cheer you on.

6. **You should picture the payoff!** Part of reaching a goal is being able to see it in your head. Talk to a medal-winning Olympic athlete and she'll tell you that years before she actually got there, she could see herself standing on the podium waiting for the Olympic official to place that medal around her neck. She'll say she could hear the national anthem playing and even feel the crowd's enthusiasm. She'll share how she pictured the cameras flashing around her and how she even planned what she was going to say when the "What's it like to have an Olympic medal?" interview questions were asked. Sounds crazy? How about sounds like success!

Chapter Two

Getting Past Your Old Habits

Before you bail on the whole idea of organizing your life, keep in mind that even the most together person on the planet has to work at being organized. It's an acquired skill, a learned talent. And just like learning to play the piano or sink shot after shot on the basketball court, you can train yourself to become more organized. And the cool thing is, once you've built a strong arsenal of organizational ammo into your daily routine, maintaining a totally together mind-set becomes a breeze.

Still wondering why your life isn't organized? Could be you're focusing on the frustration of not being on the ball rather than on the organizational efforts that'll help you accomplish your goals. Get over the idea that being organized is stuffy and boring and start to see it as something that frees you up to focus on the stuff you love most.

Are you worried that you'll end up suffering from a severe case of Martha Stewart Syndrome? It's not gonna happen, because the best organizational plan is one that's completely personalized. What works for Martha most likely isn't what will work best for you!

Rather than attempting to give your entire life a major makeover, think about a particular area of your life that you'd like to have more under control. Maybe your room is a complete mess or your grades aren't where you want 'em. Could be you'd like to save some money for a new outfit or even get a fund going so you can buy yourself a computer. Pick the area you want to work on most and turn to it first. As a particular area of your life starts to run smoother because of the new way you've chosen to operate, you'll be psyched to apply the same strategies to other areas, too.

A couple of definite Don'ts to be aware of:

Don't take on the world. The way to make headway is with small steps. Even if today's accomplishment is finding the pair of shoes you plan to wear when you go out tomorrow, at least you've accomplished your goal. If what you hope to tackle seems too huge, you need to break it down into manageable parts. Ever heard about the guy who ate a whole salami? How'd he do it? One bite at a time!

Don't put off making progress. Every small step you take will bring you closer to your goal. Even if you think today's step is a baby step, it's still better than not moving forward at all — you're that much closer to where you want to be than before you took the step. Would you rather end the day saying to yourself, "Well, I may not have done all that much, but I did take that tiny first step," or "Shoot, another day went by and I didn't do anything to get closer to my goal."

Don't convince yourself that you can't make any progress. Negative thinking is not allowed. Trade that in for an I-can-make-it-happen mind-set. Because the critical voice in your head that always seems to offer a running commentary on absolutely everything is going to bring you down. If what you're hearing is nearly all negative, hit the STOP button. And come up with a new, upbeat tune!

Maybe Tomorrow, Maybe Someday. Are you one of those people who tends to blow off responsibilities and other stuff until the last possible minute? You know the type — those who say, "Never do today what you can put off until tomorrow." Well, why *not* today? Could be you tend to procrastinate. By taking a peek at your procrastination methods, you can learn how to turn around those wait-till-tomorrow tendencies and make some major improvements today.

If you are the Crown Princess of Procrastination, here are some pointers for putting off putting things off:

Procrastination Pointer #1

On your mark, get set, go! Still stuck at the starting gate? Well, you are going to have to just get started. Make a list. Take one step. Begin at the beginning. Even the most massive task becomes more manageable when you break it down into smaller parts. Familiar with physics? One of its fundamental rules is that a body in motion tends to stay in motion. So what does that have to do with you? If you get up and get going, you're likely to keep up the pace and end up getting stuff done. Still not convinced? Make yourself a deal. Do one thing to get the ball rolling. Say you want to clean your room — rather than staring at the square footage your mom's dubbed a disaster area and getting totally discouraged, plump up those pillows and make your bed. Feel better already, don't you? Your study area is downright scary? Grab that pencil cup and throw out all the stubby pencils and outta-ink pens. That wasn't so painful, was it? And it's a start!

Procrastination Pointer #2

Start the clock. Grab that alarm clock by your bed and set it so it'll go off in fifteen minutes. Then get to the task at hand . . . studying those Spanish vocab words or folding your basket of laundry. When the alarm goes off, you're off duty. Fifteen minutes of productive time has been logged. Well done!

Procrastination Pointer #3

Offer yourself a reward. You'd love to have an ice-cream sundae? Go ahead. But first make yourself a bargain. You're only allowed the hot fudge after you're honestly able to cross something off your to-do list. You told your dad you'd drag in the trash cans from the driveway? Go get 'em and then you get to indulge.

Procrastination Pointer #4

Bribe your brother. Make a bet with someone in your household that you're gonna get a particular job done. You might even want to up the ante to make sure you hop to the task. Tell your bro you'll do his chores around the house for the next three days if you don't do what you've set out to do for yourself. The idea of signing on for his work and enduring him bugging you about how much free time he suddenly has is sure to get you moving!

Procrastination Pointer #5

Veg out. Tell yourself it's acceptable not to tackle what needs doing . . . but only if the only other thing you allow yourself to do is absolutely nothing. So you don't want to hammer away at that history homework? Fair enough. Go sit in a chair and do nothing. Before long you'll become beyond-bored so fast that you'll almost be eager to sit down and spend some time with that textbook!

Take Control of the Clock

Another way to put a lid on that nasty little habit of letting time slip away? Reclaim it by taking advantage of every available moment. You may not even realize how much valuable time you're wasting and how easy it can be to use time to your benefit instead. Even that dreaded downtime when you're cooped up in a car pool or waiting at the orthodontist can be put to good use. Here are some great ways to take advantage of those mismanaged minutes:

Perfect Timing

☀ If you feel as if you have to be up and running as soon as you get out of bed in the morning because you are forever behind schedule, try getting up fifteen minutes earlier each day. It'll give you a chance to have some breakfast . . . while actually sitting down at the breakfast table!

☀ Never have time for breakfast? Bad move. Breakfast is the most important meal of the day. Even if you don't have time for a sit-down meal, why not get in the habit of choosing a movable feast? Set out a bagel and a banana the night before. Even if you're running late, you can grab 'em as you go out the door.

☀ Do you seriously stress every morning over what you're going to wear? Why not set out an outfit the night before? Include every element, top to bottom. Too rehearsed? Put together a couple of options before you go to bed and in the morning you can choose to suit up in the outfit that suits you best.

☀ Never know where your backpack is in the morning? Designate a spot in the house where it lives. Hanging on the back of a chair. Parked in the corner near the front door. Whatever. Just get into the habit of always making sure it's there before you go to bed and, come morning, you're good to go ... not running around frantically searching for your pack as the bus drives off to school without you.

☀ Gotta bring in that permission slip for the field trip? You promised your friend she could borrow one of your CDs? Put a Post-it at eye level on the door you depart from each morning or stick it on your backpack. Put it in a place that you can't miss seeing in the morning. It'll serve as just the prompt you need to pick up that particular item.

☀ When you're waiting for the bus to show up, do some stretches or isometric exercises for a mini-workout.

☀ On that bus ride to school, why not make a list of things you need to complete your project for science class, or review your notes from yesterday's first-period class.

☀ If you're part of a car pool and everyone's taking the same language class, consider popping in a language cassette. You can turn your trip to school into a review session for Spanish class. Another option? Pop in a book-on-tape of that classic you're reading for English class. Turn drive-time into story-time and leave some of that reading to someone else. Just sit back and listen. You can play the same cassettes on your Walkman if you hoof it to school instead.

✹ If you're in charge of getting dinner together a couple of nights a week, why not make it easier on yourself (and everybody involved) by sticking to a set menu? If you're on for Friday, make it pizza night, and if it's your turn to prepare on Wednesday, why not serve up spaghetti each time? It makes shopping for ingredients and preparing a whole lot easier.

✹ After you've helped clear the dishes and before you leave the kitchen, whip up your brown bag lunch for the next day. It'll keep you from staging an A.M. freak-out because you don't have time to make lunch.

✹ Have to wait a while before it's your turn to sit in the orthodontist's chair? Take along a textbook and get some of your homework done while you wait.

✹ Before you go all the way to the mall to get those shoes that are on sale, call to see if they still have them and if they're available in your size.

Chapter Three

Money Matters

OK, so you're probably getting the picture that a lot of getting organized has to do with getting a grip on your time. In a perfect world, people would spend their time like money. As in, very carefully. While time's a commodity, so is your cold hard cash. Not sure how to handle your dough? Read on and clue in to becoming cash advanced.

You've heard the expression "Money talks"? Well, if it really did, here's what it would say:

Create a budget — rethink what it is you're doing with your dollars. Why not view your attitude toward accumulating cash as an investment system? And, as you may have guessed, what you'll be investing in is yourself. (More on this later!)

One of the best habits you can get into, and one that will serve you well for years to come, is to keep two separate cash stashes — one that you're allowed to tap into for everyday needs and immediate use and one that you vow to yourself as being absolutely off-limits.

What will that do for you? Say you sock away twenty-five dollars a month in an interest-earning account at the bank. Then you just hang around for several years. (You're planning to anyway, right?) Well, with the magic trick known as compounding, your money will be earning interest while you wait. And, over time, those small contributions will grow into some big-time bucks. Like thousands! Wanna be a millionaire? Stash away one hundred dollars a month in an account that earns around eight percent interest (such as a mutual fund) and by the time you are around the age of your parents, you'll be able to call yourself one — a millionaire, that is. All because of the cool concept called compounding. Which basically translates to: The younger you are when you start stashing your cash, the sooner you'll be able to call yourself an incredibly wealthy woman! Time is on your side. In a big way!

Investing: The Long and Short of It

Investing is a way to make money *with* your money. But first you need to have the money to invest. Maybe you get an allowance, or your grandma always sends you a check on your birthday, or you baby-sit the little kids next door. Start saving the cash you get right away. The earlier you start saving, and the earlier you turn saving into investing, the more time you're giving your money to *earn* money. Make a point of stashing away cash on a regular basis. Even if it's just a buck a week every Friday, that adds up to fifty-two dollars a year. Then the next step is to make your money grow through investing.

First you'll want to decide on some financial goals. Then divide them into two groups. Short-term goals — things that you need or want as soon as you can get them, such as a bike, computer, or CD player. Then come up with a couple of long-term goals — things that you think you'll need or want a few years down the road, like money for college, funds to travel around Europe, or cash for a new car once you get your license. Generally, these long-term goals are seriously expensive and require some advance planning. It might sound crazy to start thinking about stuff that seems so far away, but the earlier you start investing, the sooner you'll reach your financial goals. A small sum invested right now will grow over time.

Is This Risky Business?

Investing allows your money to grow, but the flip side is that there *are* some risks involved with investing. Ideally, you should be investing in a way that minimizes risks and maximizes your rewards. Luckily, there are some investment options that are less risky than others if you'd prefer to play it safe. The most important thing is simply to get in the habit of saving. Here are three options:

You can put your money in a savings account or a CD (certificate of deposit) account at a bank or financial institution. Banks, savings and loans, and credit unions have always been viewed as good places to open up accounts to start saving. The return on your savings is usually at a rate of about two to five percent. Even though these returns may strike you as kind of small, this type of investment provides a safe place to park your money. These types of accounts are also usually pretty convenient to open up and easy to add to. A CD will earn you more interest than a savings account; but once you put a certain amount of money in a CD — say one thousand dollars — you can't take it out for a set amount of time in order to get the interest (say, six months at five percent interest).

You can buy shares of stock. If the idea of owning part of a company sounds appealing, you may want to look into buying a share, or shares, of stock. Even though you're under eighteen, you can still get involved with the stock market. You will need one of your parents to buy the stock for you through a stockbroker and place it in a custodial account. Then, once you hit eighteen, you can buy stock in your own name. Lots of companies now allow you to invest directly through direct stock purchase plans; you can typically buy additional shares after you've made an initial investment.

It's a cool way to feel connected to the company — but it can be risky. If the company does well, you're likely to see the value of your shares of stock go up, but if the company takes a hit, so do your shares! So make sure you're ready to take chances before you buy stock.

It would also be a good idea to learn more about stocks, bonds, and mutual funds before getting involved — a great book geared for kids is *Growing Money: A Complete Investing Guide for Kids* by Gail Karlitz, Debbie Honig, and Stephen Lewis (illustrator). Look for it in your local bookstore, library, or through Amazon.com. A great Web site to check out for investment info is called Investing for Kids. This site has a stock game, stock learning center, information on kid-friendly investment ideas, plus a glossary of terms — to help you get started! The Web address is: http://tqd.advanced.org/3096/

You can invest in mutual funds. When you invest in a mutual fund, it's as if you're purchasing lots of different shares of stock from lots of different companies along with lots of other people. A fund manager makes the decisions. This manager invests pooled money that people have contributed, so he or she has a bigger amount to invest with. It can be riskier than simply letting your money sit in a savings account, but the payoff can be much more rewarding. If the mutual fund does well, so do you. And it's much less risky than just buying one stock because even if the stock of one particular company that's part of the mutual fund goes down, the other companies can balance it out.

Other Money Tips

☀ Don't just pocket your profits — earmark what you're earning in interest for something special. Maybe it'll pay for your first car or fund a trip to France during your junior year of college. Picture what that money will pay for and saving will take on more meaning to you.

☀ Read up on companies that interest you. If you're buying stock in a company, you probably believe in it. Peter Lynch, a famous guy in the world of finance, made a major amount of money by listening to what his daughters had to say about certain brands and watching what store bags they brought home from the mall. Buying Gap stock, for example, scored him some serious dough. Apply the same principles yourself and it's likely to pay off for you.

☀ Familiarize yourself with the financial section of the newspaper. Sure, it looks pretty whacked-out, but if you get to know the symbols and terminology you'll be setting yourself up for a profitable future.

☀ Talk to your parents if they make a lot of investments and ask them to share some of their smarts with you.

☀ Study financial vocab words the same way you would for a French class. Once you've got 'em learned, you'll be more fluent in the world of finance.

☀ Read up to learn more about budgeting and saving your money. Two good books are: *Moneymakers: Good Cents for Girls* by Ingrid Roper and Susan Synarski (illustrator); and *The Money Book and Hideaway Bank* by Elaine Wyatt and Stan Hinden (illustrated by Arnie Levin). Both books are geared toward young

people and feature tips and hints about earning, budgeting, spending, and saving your
money.

Can't seem to collect enough coinage to fill
up that piggy bank's little potbelly? Here are a
couple of cool, simple tricks that'll help you
turn a pocketful of pennies into serious moola
and help you stick with a savings strategy:

☀ Every time you buy something, keep the
change. If a magazine is $2.50, pay for it with
three dollars and keep the change you get
back for your savings stash. The cool thing
about this trick is that you can keep track of
your spending using full dollar amounts. In
your mind, think of every purchase you make
as a full dollar amount. (That magazine cost
you three bucks.) You'll have the change from
each purchase to add to your savings.

☀ See it to believe it. If you put your
money into a piggy bank but don't feel you're
seeing any progress, make the switch to a
clear container. You'll see the funds fill up.
Also, you may want to place a sticker on each
savings jar that states what you're saving for.

It's a good idea to have one stash for long-term investing and one for more near-future goals. The contents of one jar can go straight to the bank and the contents of the other can go toward purchasing something you want right away. If you deprive yourself of absolutely everything, you might give up on the whole savings system and that's not where you want to be.

Bring on the Budget

All this saving and investing sounds good, but what if you just can't seem to save your dough? Could be you need to set up a budget. Sure, it may not sound too fun at first but if you want to get some savings going, it's something you'll have to do.

How to do it? Try this. Get yourself a super-small spiral notebook. Then, absolutely *every time* you spend even a cent, write it down. Say you're at the counter of a convenience store buying a pack of gum and a soda. As soon as you pull out your wallet to pay for your purchases, whip out a pencil and log in what it is you're buying and how much you're spending (the grand total, tax included). Okay, so maybe this is gonna get old real fast — fair enough. But the benefits definitely outweigh the annoyance. Taking the time to track where your money goes will allow you to see what you're spending (wasting?) your money on and will enable you to focus on which purchases you truly need and which are wastes of money. Think spending a dollar a day at the soda machine is no big deal? Think again — that adds up to $365 a year that could definitely be better spent on something way more useful. By limiting your purchases to what you need, you'll be able to put some cash away to save.

Still can't seem to figure out where all that money's going? You've been careful not to spend your cash on a bunch of impulse purchases but are still left with nothing? Well, it could be you don't have a real awareness of how much of your money is already earmarked for (and being eaten up by) fixed expenses. To figure this out, take the time at the beginning of each month (each week if that works better for you) to jot down the expenses you *know* you're going to incur (club dues, music or dance lessons, bus fare to school) and put cash aside for those expenses right away.

You have to keep close track of all your expenses (not just your purchases) to really be able to cut back on spending and start saving.

Making Sense of Your Spending

Next to each entry below, write down how much you spend on the item or items per month. If you don't know for sure, make a good guess. After a month of keeping close track of all purchases, compare what you *really* spent to your estimates. You'll probably find you're spending more than you think.

If you want to begin saving, figure out how much you can spend per month in order to still have some cash left over afterward to put in your savings account. Then you'll have to budget this money across the expenses that are really essential.

Here are some potential money eater-uppers:

⚙ Clothing

⚙ Hair and beauty products

⚙ Club dues

- Music/dance/sports lessons

- Magazines, books, and subscriptions

- Commuting and transportation costs

- School supplies

- Gifts for holidays and birthdays

- Eating out

- Movie tickets and food

- Gear and supplies for sports and hobbies

The trick isn't to give up absolutely everything you spend money on that makes your life interesting. Just opt for putting a little more financial focus on a couple of categories where you're willing to cut back on your spending so that you can be sure you have enough money available at the end of each month to invest.

Chapter Four

Conquering Clutter: The Room Redo

Tired of forging your way through your room in an attempt to crash on your bed? While your room *is* Sleep Central, it also serves as a place for storing tons of your stuff. If you're interested in making the most of the space available, set yourself up with some serious storage capabilities — and strategies! A good way to get a handle on what you've got is to ask yourself a lot of questions. The way you answer 'em can help you determine how to organize your space.

Ask Yourself, "How Can This Cleanup Help Others?"

A big part of starting a room redo is psyching yourself up for the task at hand. So spending the day cleaning your room isn't exactly at the top of your chart? Fair enough. But the thing is, by gearing up to get rid of stuff, you will literally lighten your load. That feels good. Not convinced? Look at it this way. A totally positive component to consider is that when you gather up the stuff that you no longer need, you'll probably end up donating some of it to charity. So in your effort to do something for yourself, you'll be helping out others, too. Suddenly what was looking like giving up stuff is all about giving TO others. Nice job!

Ask Yourself, "Should It Stay or Should It Go?"

With some stuff, you'll want to say, "Stay." With other stuff, you'll be shouting, "Sayonara!" While you will want to take a hard look at the stuff stashed in your room, you won't want to look at it all at once! Sure, you've gotta know what you're dealing with, but you don't want to completely overwhelm yourself. Fleeing your room with your arms flapping at your sides is not the solution. Instead, pick a portion of your closet or a dresser drawer and just deal with your room one small section at a time. In a couple of weeks, you'll have conquered the whole space!

Ask Yourself, "Is It Behind Door Number One or Door Number Two?"

Each and every item that earns a place in your room should fall into one of two categories — Something You Use or Something You Treasure. Pick up that sweater and say to yourself, "Do I wear this a lot?" If the answer isn't an affirmative, it's time for it to go. In the other category, you might have a pretty locket that you never, ever wear, but it was given to you by your grandmother. That's the kind of thing you want to hold on to.

Closet Cleanup

OK, you've just entered the wardrobe department. Are you ready for a clothes encounter? Why not whittle your wardrobe down to the stuff you really wear? Get your shoes sorted and organize all those accessories. Here's how: *Take a good hard look at the stuff you've got.*

What's next? Here are the goals for the girl who wants to know all about her wardrobe:

Divide and Conquer

Categorize your clothes. Most likely there's some stuff you wear often (think jeans) and some stuff you may not slip into every day of the week (think swimsuit). So try to divide your clothes into different categories. Designate a section of your clothing storage space to your workout clothes, another to the clothes you wear to school each week, another to your after-school and weekend clothes, and finally have a smaller section for stuff you wear only on special occasions.

While you're at it, if you have a younger sibling, set aside some stuff that she might be interested in inheriting from you. Also, while you're sorting, set up a box or bag that's the place for clothes you plan to give to charity. If you have old clothes that are really ratty, they should go in the garbage or you can always rip 'em up to use as cleaning rags!

If you're still finding it difficult to get with the get-organized-or-give-it-away program, here are some all-important questions worth asking:

"Will I ever wear this again?"

If the answer is no, donate the item. Otherwise, odds are it's just gonna end up stuffed in the back of your closet.

"Does this go with other stuff I have?"

If you can't mentally picture at least a couple of things you have that you can wear it with, it's not really a part of your WORKING wardrobe. It may be one to get rid of.

"How long has it been since I've worn it? Why?"

It's been six months since you last wore it? How come? There's a hole in the fabric? It no longer fits? It's out of style? You were planning to give it to your cousin? Decide to act.

"Does this look good on me?"

When you saw it at the mall, it looked adorable. When you bought and brought it home, you had second thoughts and you've never really worn it out in public. What makes you think you're going to change your mind? If it was a mall mistake, let it go. Letting it take up crucial closet space isn't going to make you want to wear it.

"Is this comfortable?"

It's a completely cool cargo skirt but you've always hated the way it bunches up at your waist. And when you sit down it seriously sinks into your sides. Rather than wasting time thinking about the pain a particular piece of clothing puts you through, give it away to someone who won't be affected by it in the same way.

"How many other items just like it do I have?"

When those sweats went on sale, you bought a pair in every color under the sun and now you're kind of sick of the style? Why not keep a couple of pairs in your fave shades and expand your storage space by getting rid of the others?

"Does this sock have a mate?"

You know its partner has probably entered that weird black hole in the laundry area where single socks decide to reside by themselves. Unless you plan to use your Herculean strength to lift up the washer and dryer and look underneath for the sock that's missing in action, it may be time to turn the other part of the pair into a handy little dusting mitt.

"Do these nylons have any runs?"

Why is it when the runs are near the toes you figure you can kind of twist and turn the hose into an interesting shape and still get a couple of wears out of 'em? Give it up. And if you're talking major runs up your leg, we're here to tell you that's tacky. Toss 'em or cut 'em up and use 'em as hair ties.

"Is this too much trouble to wear?"

Yes, it's a great outfit. But every time you wear it (which isn't that often) you have to do some major ironing, press a bunch of pleats, and be careful not to spill anything on it because the dry-cleaning bill causes your mom to freak. Could be this wardrobe wonder is just a tad too high-maintenance.

1. Only keep stuff you really will wear. If the fabric is worn, an item has lost its shape, has stains that just won't come out, or is faded to the point of no return, the jury says, "Jettison!"

2. If an item is fixable, fix it! A missing button can be sewn on while you watch a sitcom. A hem can be let out easily enough. If you don't plan to put in the time to mend something, put it in a box or bag of stuff that's moving out.

3. If you have a laundry bag or hamper in your room, consider adding a charity bag to the mix. When you're ready to rid yourself of a good garment that no longer suits your style, you'll know exactly where it goes. Also, if you're a serious shopper, try to keep your closet under control with this handy trick: When something new enters the closet, make a point of having something old that you no longer wear leave. The stuff that should earn a spot

in your closet is the stuff that really gets worn. Other items are just taking up space.

Clothes Quarters

Want to work wonders on your wardrobe? Here's a quick list of ways to keep track of your clothes:

⚘ Plastic or wicker baskets: The perfect storage space for socks, underwear, leotards, and tights.

⚘ Clear plastic shoe boxes: Excellent because they allow you a sneak peek at what's inside without having to open 'em up.

⚘ Mesh bags: Cool for loading up with all kinds of stuff, they also make a lot of sense when it's time to do laundry.

⚘ Corkboard and pushpins: Use 'em to hang up your necklaces, hair accessories, and earrings.

⚘ Under-bed storage boxes: Great for stuff you don't use all that often.

‹※› Tiered wire baskets: Cool for hair stuff and belts and scarves.

‹※› Hanging shoe holders: Load up your shoes and be able to see the whole collection at once.

‹※› Clear plastic garment bags: Good for stuff that's special but that you don't wear all that often, such as wool coats and formal dresses.

‹※› Coatracks: Cool for heavy coats and hats.

‹※› Cabinets: Great for storing things you can fold and stack, like T-shirts and sweaters.

‹※› Dressers: A good place to park collections of smaller stuff, such as socks, underwear, and T-shirts.

‹※› Armoires: These big storage centers can house practically an entire wardrobe. Most are equipped with a rack for hanging items and drawers for stuff you can fold. These are particularly great if you're lacking in closet space.

‹※› Padded hangers: Handy for clothes made of delicate fabrics because the padding is gentler, and also great for dresses that have skinny straps because the hangers' material helps garments stay put.

⊛ Trunks: Good for long-term storage of stuff you don't wear all that often and for things that are super-sentimental.

⊛ Plastic footlockers: Put athletic gear here.

⊛ Plastic or wooden mug rack: Hang scarves, necklaces, belts, and bandanas from these.

⊛ Pegboard: You can get hooked on these as a solution for storing jewelry and hair accessories.

⊛ Plastic crates: A cool place for casual clothes, like sweats, and also for stashing shoes.

How's Your Bedside Manner?

When you step out of bed in the morning, what are the odds that you'll step on something scary? Did you set down that slice of veggie pizza when you were snacking yesterday afternoon and now it's squished between your toes as you head off to hit the showers?

That's kinda gross. Sounds like you could use some help.

To make the best of the space around where you sleep, station a bedside table, dresser, or bookshelf near the head of your bed. If it has a drawer, you've got the perfect place to stash a flashlight for when you're hearing those suspicious straight-out-of-*Scream* noises and a great place to keep a pad of paper and a pen (for jotting down interesting ideas or detailing that really weird dream). And guess what? The dresser will serve as the all-important resting place for that plate with the cold pizza slice. The bedside location should be for stuff you use often. If there's something sitting there that you don't use at least a couple of times a week, it's parked in the wrong place!

Under your bed is a great place for long-term storage stash. Ski season's over? An under-the-bed storage box is a great spot for your goggles, ski gloves, and other ski gear. The suitcases you stash for summer vacations are good to go under the bed, too. But be smart about it and pack 'em with stuff before you slide them into position. There's no sense letting that lazy luggage go into hibernation without helping you to create the ultimate organized room. Turn it into a hidden asset!

Are Your Hobbies Holding You Back?

If you could spend your time doing exactly what you want, odds are you would get super-involved in some of your favorite sports and hobbies. Cool enough. But be honest with yourself. Are you still as into some of the stuff that rocked your world a year ago? Chances are some of your interests have changed and others have you more involved than ever. This section is all about figuring out which stuff is still of interest and which projects, supplies, and tools are about due for a relocation package.

Some of your interests, especially crafts, may not be things you do every day. So, you guessed it, you're gonna want to find a place for those projects to live when you're not us-ing 'em. Here are some instant organizers worth considering:

☀ A case or toolbox that houses the main tools for your hobby. If you're totally into scrapbooking, why not stash your stuff in a "portable office" file box? It's got room for scissors, pens, stickers, and file folders for photos and papers you're likely to use. Plastic shoe or sweater boxes also make great storage centers.

☀ A rolling cart can house even more craft gear. Look for 'em at art supply stores or in the closet and storage section of most chain stores.

☀ Into making your own jewelry? Why not get one of those completely compartmentalized boxes used for storing embroidery thread? Tackle boxes designed for fishing can help you keep track of all your beads, too.

☀ Completely into cooking? Instead of the rip-and-tear method of adding new recipes to your to-try pile, why not insert 'em into a three-ring binder?

☀ If you're an Earth girl and want to do your part to protect the planet, rethink the stuff you recycle. Could be they can live a new life helping you get a handle on your hobby. Old oatmeal boxes, small glass jars with lids, and empty coffee cans with plastic lids are all great for stashing your stuff.

sweater boxes also make great storage centers.

b A rolling cart can house even more craft gear. Look for 'em at art supply stores or in the closet and storage section of most chain stores.

b Into making your own jewelry? Why not get one of those completely compartmentalized boxes used for storing embroidery thread? Tackle boxes designed for fishing can help you keep track of all your beads, too.

b Completely into cooking? Instead of the rip-and-tear method of adding new recipes to your to-try pile, why not insert 'em into a three-ring binder?

b If you're an Earth girl and want to do your part to protect the planet, rethink the stuff you recycle. Could be they can live a new life helping you get a handle on your hobby. Old oatmeal boxes, small glass jars with lids, and empty coffee cans with plastic lids are all great for stashing your stuff.

b Gone berserk over Beanie Babies and other collectibles? Think about storing them tion. Second, make your bed already. If your bed is made, the whole room looks better. Odds are strong that your bed is one of the biggest objects in your room. So if it's looking together, it'll do wonders for the rest of your room. Third, grab everything that's on the floor into one massive pile. Give yourself five minutes to put away as much of it as you can. Toss the rest of it in the closet. Spritz the room with some aromatherapy spray or your favorite scent. Voilà! Instant room makeover!

Shared Space Solutions

So you've got your personal space under control? Why not make a huge contribution to the entire household by setting up some seriously organized spaces in areas everybody uses? After all, you'll benefit from a more together household and you're likely to score some big brownie points with the parents as well! How to do it? Check out these room redos for the rest of the house:

TV Central

Why not set up a storage system for videos, video games, and CDs? You can start with shoe boxes! Use 'em to organize CDs, alphabetically by artist or group names or by category (Rock, Classical, etc.) or by the person they belong to (Dad's, Mom's, Mine). A similar system can be set up for videos. You can create your own baby Blockbuster by categorizing movie videos, too (Action, Comedy, Exercise, Suspense, Girl Flicks).

A Battle-free Bathroom

If you share a bathroom (or even if you're lucky enough to have one all to yourself), there are some ways you can keep from being buried alive by shampoo bottles and blow-dryers. Since bathrooms are usually the tiniest rooms in the house, it's a challenge to store all that stuff that's meant to keep you clean and cute. The secret is using lots of organizers. Add a storage shelf or shower caddy to the shower stall. It can be home for all those bottles of shampoo and conditioner. It also will offer a spot for bath sponges and shower gel. House all your hair stuff in one drawer or storage area, including blow-dryer, brushes, combs, barrettes, headbands, mousses, and clips. Create a similar shelf for everything to do with dental health (toothbrushes, tubes of toothpaste, dental floss, your retainer, etc.).

Another way to better organize the bathroom is by doing a quick inventory of all the lotions and potions that are currently taking up space. Think about all those half-used bottles of beauty aids that you don't really like anymore. Some of them are probably so old that they've lost their scent! Here's the rule: If you're not using it anymore, out it goes! If in a week's time you are despondent about that deodorant you threw out, you can always go to the local drugstore and buy another one.

Still feeling as if there's just not enough space? Why not add a hanging mesh basket (the kind that's designed to be used for produce) in the bathroom and use it as a caddy for cosmetics and stuff that gets you clean?

Chapter Five

School, Studying, and the Great Paper Chase

Get Smart about Studying

Putting in megahours cramming right before a test isn't the way to become successful in school. Studies show that the best way to take in info is in small bites. In fact, if you stare at that subject matter for more than two hours straight, you've probably lost your edge. There are ways you can improve your study style — and last time we checked, that generally translates to improving your grades.

One of the first things to focus on is finding out how you learn best. The way people learn falls into different categories. Wanna know where you fall? If you're part of the pack, you learn best visually. Fifty percent of students absorb info by seeing, reading, and remembering what they've seen. Not your style? Could be you're an auditory learner. Huh? You heard right. Auditory students learn best by listening. You tend to remember what a teacher has said and probably do best in classes in which the teachers lecture a lot. If you're assigned a complete heap of homework to read, you're the one who's most likely to lose interest after about ten minutes.

If neither of these types of learners sounds like you, it could be 'cause you're a kinesthetic learner, which means you're action-oriented. You excel in learning environments where you get to handle and hold things. Chances are you love doing lab work or putting parts together. You learn by doing.

So how will knowing what kind of learner you are help you get a better grip on your grades? If you're a visual learner, your Study Smart style should include reviewing your notes and reading over your textbooks. Once you see things spelled out, you tend to succeed. Read up on everything for maximum results.

If you're an auditory learner, your Study Smart style should include thinking back on what was said in class and going over comments your teacher made. Jot down notes to trigger your mind back to what your teacher was talking about, and talk things out as you study. Studying with a bud is also helpful. The two of you can quiz each other out loud because once you hear something, you hardly ever forget it.

If you're a kinesthetic learner, your Study Smart style should include getting a feel for the subject matter through hands-on learning. When there aren't lots of opportunities to learn this way, you can come up with some manual aids of your own. Studying the geography of a particular region? Why not draw your own map to make that hand-eye-brain connection you need to most effectively grasp important info? Hands-on learning is what works for you, so if you can come up with some handy ways to learn, use them!

Every Day Can Make a Difference

Want some study tips to use in the classroom every day? By using these strategies, come test time, you'll already have things under control.

Read everything on the page. Instead of just focusing on the text, pay attention to the charts, captions, and pictures that appear on the page, too. These sections often contain valuble information in an easy-to-understand (and easier-to-remember) format.

Speak up. Teachers love when students participate in class. The cool thing about speaking up in class is that it makes class more interesting. Plus, you get a chance to express your thoughts and opinions. Also, if you end up on the border between a B+ and an A- when it comes time for the teacher to give out the grades, your instructor is way more likely to swing the vote in your favor if you are a participator because he or she will think of you as someone who contributed to and made a real effort in class.

Build Yourself a Blissed-out Study Space

The area where you set yourself up to study should serve as one of your main study aids. Rather than working in some little corner that's cluttered and confining, strive to set up a space that's seriously serene. Think of it as your Zen den. A place you park yourself to study that actually leaves you with a relaxed, focused mind-set. Sound impossible? It's not. Here are some ways you can increase the peace by simplifying your study space and setting yourself up for a soothing experience:

☀ First keep the area where you study clean. Big piles of papers at your elbows aren't gonna help you concentrate. An in basket or a file cabinet with folders for each of the subjects you're studying will help you to keep track of things for the whole school term.

☀ If you work on a computer, select a computer screensaver that's super-soothing. Rather than a bunch of fish that eat one another, choose a scenic shot or a passage from a poem you like. It will remind you that it's best to be in a mellow mood when you're working on stuff that's building up your brain.

✷ Play some classical music as you study. The tunes can take away your tension, and some studies have shown that certain types of classical music can actually help your brain retain more information. So make room for Mozart! Reading while classical music is playing in the background has been shown to boost comprehension. And there's evidence that proves listening to Mozart can raise your IQ! What makes the notes so worthy? The music can help you concentrate, filter out distracting noise, prolong your attention span, and help you to encode information so that you store it better in your brain. Think of 'em as sonatas that sharpen your mind! Try listening to Mozart's Piano Concerto, No. 17 Finale, or Johann Sebastian Bach's Prelude and Fugue No. 1. Both have been linked with helping to stimulate thinking and encourage recall of material. Sounds pretty good, doesn't it?

✷ Consider placing a plant on your desk. That natural element will help put you at ease even on those nights when you feel you're being buried alive by homework. How does it work? The scientific term for connecting with nature is biophilia. By adding some natural elements to your study space, you can reduce your anxiety level and lower your blood pressure. Last time you checked you didn't have a green thumb? Not to worry. There are some plants that are pretty much impossible to do in. Why not add a snake plant to your study space? It has flat, hard, glossy leaves that grow straight up. It doesn't need direct sunlight and you only have to water it once a week. The spider plant is another good pick. It needs bright light and you water it only once a week. Chinese evergreen is another water-it-once-a-week-and-forget-about-it plant. And aloe is a cool choice because it can also serve as a small first-aid station when you experience one of those nasty paper cuts. Just snap off a little piece of the plant and place it on the cut for soothing relief. It needs direct sunlight and you water it every two weeks.

☀ Adjust your attitude with aromatherapy. A small diffuser or a ring that can be placed around the lightbulb of a lamp can hold some essential oil that'll scent your space with a soothing fragrance. Lavender, vanilla, jasmine, and ylang-ylang are said to be some of the most soothing scents to choose from. Not up for the full-on fragrance setup? Add a tiny drop or two of your favorite soothing essential oil to a little bit of canola oil (straight out of the kitchen cupboard) and smooth it onto your earlobes or your temples as a meditative mini-study break.

Study Station Stuff

Everybody has their own study style, and chances are you've found a strategy that works for you. One of the tricks to acing all things academic is to have a stash of the key tools of the trade. While you probably don't need everything on this list to see results, there may be some items you could add to your study station that'll help you make the grade!

- ✸ Desk or sturdy counter or tabletop for writing
- ✸ Good lighting
- ✸ Calculator
- ✸ Wastebasket
- ✸ Bulletin board, corkboard, or dry-erase board

- Clock
- Computer
- Notebook paper
- Dictionary
- Thesaurus
- Scratch paper
- Self-stick notes
- Pens that work
- Sharp pencils
- Pencil sharpener
- Eraser
- Stapler
- Staple remover
- Tape
- Scissors
- Highlighters
- Paper clips
- Hole punch
- Colored file folders
- Stackable or upright filing tray

Instant Upgrades: Three Tools of the Trade That Are Worth a Try

While a pencil and some paper can go a long way to helping you do well in class, here are three big-ticket items that can give you a serious academic edge:

A computer

Not everyone has instant access to a computer. If you don't have one at home, check out your local library and look into logging on there. Or hang out at your school's study center if it has computers available for use.

Internet access

Surfing out stuff on the World Wide Web is like having an entire library at your fingertips. It's amazing for helping you find out facts for a research paper or taking a virtual tour of a museum or college campus you've always been curious about. Again, if the Internet isn't something that's right under your roof, there are libraries, community centers, and even cafés that offer access by the hour.

A tape recorder

Can't live without your Walkman when it comes to listening to music? Cool enough. But how about investing in a small tape recorder to help you "take notes" in class?

While jotting things down in class is always important, if you tape-record lectures as well, then by pressing the PLAY button when you get home you'll be able to listen to what went on in class all over again and pick up any points you may have missed. Or you can just review the material for better recall later during test time. Also, when you're working out or taking a bus, car, or train ride, you can make use of your time by listening to important info all over again. Some teachers don't allow the tape-recording of class, so check with yours first to see if it's all right.

Do You Compute?

You're all over the Internet? You e-mail everybody? Cool deal. But are you as on-line-organized as you could be? Here's some *Get It Together* advice that'll have you surfing in style.

One of the things those computer guru types were hoping to create with computers was a world without so much paper. Think they pulled it off? Not! How can you help make your world a little less piled up with paper? When you're working away at your computer keyboard, ask yourself some questions:

Can I work with what I have on-screen?
Do I need to save this version?
Will I really refer to this again?
Can I throw this on a disk instead of printing it out on paper?

Even if you're able to demonstrate some restraint by not printing out reams of paper, you can still wind up with a phenomenal number of completely confusing computer files. How to get a grip? Set up a first-rate computer file system the first time out. To keep from having a far-too-many-files freak-out, get rid of files you don't need anymore and label the ones you choose to keep in a way that will still make sense to you in a couple of weeks. Only save what you really, truly, for-sure need.

Another major time-saver? Whip out that computer manual and actually give it a read. Computers have incredible capabilities and lots of people don't tap in to all they have to offer. By reading the software manual, you'll discover all kinds of shortcuts and tricks to make things go smoother for you.

You can organize your life by creating a List File on your computer. Phone lists of friends, addresses for relatives, personal goals, and directions to places you don't go to often can all be put on lists that will help you keep track and be organized.

E-mail Extras

If you love to e-mail your friends, some of these correspondence clues can help you to save time and stay organized:

DO communicate your mood easily and quickly with these symbols:

for a smile :-)
for a frown :-(
for a wink ;-)

DO keep a list of all your pals' e-mail addresses ready at hand. Most computers have great built-in electronic address books that you can pull up right on your screen for quick access.

DO use these shortcuts for frequently used phrases to save yourself some time:

BTW = By the way
LOL = Laughing out loud
JIC = Just in case
IMO = In my opinion
CUL = Catch you later
BFN = Bye for now

And remember, never give your real name or address to someone you meet on the Internet.

The Attack of the Killer Backpack!

Feeling like you're carrying too heavy a load? Well, you're probably right! The average school backpack weighs twenty or more pounds! How to lighten your load? Empty out the nonessentials. Do you really need to carry around an extra set of sneakers? Okay, maybe. But you can part with that pile of papers from the science fair you went to a week ago, and you definitely don't need three different-flavored lip balms — one will do.

Thin out your loose-leaf binders. If you're still schlepping around assignments from last semester, it's time to remove 'em and file them away in your study area in case you need to refer to them again. Your backpack should really include only those items you might need *today*, not stuff from three months ago (or even from yesterday, if you no longer need it).

If you've got a huge hairbrush in your pack, consider making the switch to one that's smaller. Keep a couple of barrettes in a little makeup bag along with only the most essential items instead of opting for one of everything you stash at home in the bathroom. If your schedule allows for it, make a trip or two to your locker between classes to unload some of your textbooks. Then go pick 'em up before you head home. To make carrying your pack as comfortable as possible, be sure the straps are adjusted properly for your height. The bulk of your backpack's contents should rest just below your shoulder blades.

The Locker Lowdown: Four Steps for a Streamlined Space

Another key to feeling in control at school is by having an organized locker. To avoid an avalanche that buries the person who has the locker below you every time you open your locker, have a plan for how you're going to use this limited storage space. Think of it as the overhead bin on an airplane. It can be annoying to hear the flight attendants remind you of how important it is to not overload those bins but their point is a valid one. Stuffing storage spaces can be dangerous!

To avoid disaster, stage a weekly review of what you have in your locker. Maybe you brought some photos to school last week to show your friends. They've seen 'em, so now it's time to take those pictures home. How about that massive history report your teacher handed back two weeks ago? Is your locker really the best place for the report now that it's history?

There are some items you'll always want to have in your locker: extra pencils, some emergency supplies for the bathroom, maybe a T-shirt or sweatshirt in case you spill stuff on yourself at lunch or the weather takes a turn for the worse. Those are the kinds of items that a locker is meant to shelter. To keep track of the little items, add a plastic pencil box or a small makeup bag to your locker where you can stash odds and ends.

Another rule that helps keep your locker looking good? Make a pact not to put any perishable food in there! That's when things can get really gruesome.

Chapter Six

Making Time for Yourself, Your Friends, and Your Family

Time for Yourself

Set aside some time each day that's absolutely your own. Write in a journal, read a book you love, or flip through a magazine. If you can't seem to keep a date with yourself, write down a set time in your calendar. You should try to spend at least an hour each week just thinking things through. When you give yourself time to contemplate, you're more likely to sort out the silly stuff from the things that matter most to you, and then chances are you'll be more focused in life. End each day with a special ritual that's all your own. Listen to a song that has meaning to you or read a poem each night before you switch off the lamp by your bed. Heading to bed with a relaxed, mellow mind-set will help you face the next day in a better mood.

Interested in some other ways you can feel better about yourself and boost your confidence? Here are seven surefire steps to personal success:

DON'T wear an outfit that you don't feel good in. Your ultimate goal should be to only wear stuff that makes you feel great!

DO keep a journal and write down all the things you're good at. On those days when you feel like you can't do anything right, turn to those journal entries and remind yourself of all the ways in which you excel.

DO stand tall. By standing up straight you instantly convey confidence. And when others perceive you as confident, you'll see yourself in a more positive light, too. A slouched, slumped-over spine conveys that your world is caving in on you! Not the message you want to send.

DO smile at yourself in the mirror each morning. Isn't that the way you want people to see you? Cheerful and happy. See yourself that way, too, by getting a glance of your grin at the start of each day.

DO read a bio about someone you've always admired for instant inspiration. It can be anyone from Sally Ride to Julia Roberts. You're likely to find that they've overcome obstacles to get to where they are, and their success stories can inspire you to follow your goals and be a high-achiever.

DO make a point of complimenting at least one person every day. Letting others know that they've made a positive impression on you is likely to lead to hearing reciprocal complimentary stuff about you. Besides, it just feels good to bring a smile to someone's face.

DO complete one task each day that doesn't really thrill you. It can be flossing your teeth or studying grammar rules. The point is, by tackling it, you get the added blast of confidence from knowing you've taken control.

For the Health of It

Another reason it makes major sense to make time for yourself is because it allows you the time you need to take care of yourself — emotionally and physically. Establishing healthful habits now will pay off for the rest of your life. The more super-busy and crazy your life is, the more in control of your bod you'll wanna be. Hiking, playing tennis with a friend, riding your bike, swimming some laps, or shooting some hoops are all great ways to get stronger while getting rid of stress and pent-up frustrations.

Rather than obsessing about what you're gonna wear to work out, give some thought to what athletic activities you like best. If you despise jogging, you're not exactly gonna be strapping on your running shoes to race out the door each morning. Figure out which activities make you feel good. Do you think of yourself as super-competitive? Stick with the sports that you'll really get involved with and know that you'll be taking an active stand about your health and happiness!

A key to getting done everything you want to do is having enough energy to do it. The way to fuel yourself for phenomenal results is to stick with healthful food choices. That double-trouble burger with cheese and a side of fries is not going to give you the energy you need to get through the day. Some much more energetic options include:

☀ Calcium-rich dairy products made from nonfat milk

☀ Vitamin-rich fresh fruits and veggies (You should set your sites on scarfing down five servings every day.)

☀ Calcium-fortified orange juice

☀ Iron-rich fortified breakfast cereals, whole grains, and dark-green leafy veggies

☀ Protein-packed, low-in-fat legumes, such as peas, lentils, and beans

☀ Protein-rich lean meats

Make meal choices that help you run at optimum speed. No sense hitting the fast-food track and then struggling to stay awake 'cause you're being fueled by fat, sodium, and sugar. Yuck!

Time for Your Friends

If your goal is to make better use of your time, then making more time for your friends should definitely be a priority. Here's something worth remembering: People matter most. No matter how crazed your calendar becomes, you've gotta make time for your friends. How to do it without suffering from serious bud burnout? Agree to get together during a certain time each day or to set aside Saturdays for hanging out together. If your mom is making you run a bunch of errands, call up your girlfriend to see if she's willing to go along with you. It may not be the most exciting afternoon ever planned, but it'll at least give you some time together. And surely you can always spare five minutes of phone time.

The point is, no matter how busy you become, your friends have to know that they are a high priority to you. Make a point of connecting with your pals each day. A phone call or a quick convo in the hallway at school will go a long way toward conveying that you care about 'em.

Another way to make sure you don't have to choose between your *amigas* and all the other things you need to get done is to do some of that stuff while you're on the phone. Think about saving up for a cordless phone (or maybe there's already one in the house) so you can walk around and water some houseplants or do other chores as you talk on the phone. You can tidy up your room, chop up vegetables for dinner, or set the table while you share the day's dirt with your best bud. Another option is an extra-long extension cord so you don't feel confined to a particular space when you're on the phone.

An Organized Girl's Guide to Gift-giving

If you've got a whole crew of companions, one of the things that can lead to social-life stress is the big-time birthday-gift buying scene. Does this leave you present tense? Check out these gift-buying guidelines and you'll never be caught empty-handed!

✸ Make a list of possible presents for each of your pals. Keep an ongoing list for all buds, even if their birthdays aren't anytime soon. That way, when the date arrives, or during the winter holidays, you'll have a few ideas to choose from. Make sure you're not spending too much.

✸ Keep a page in a notebook for jotting down gift ideas as they come to you. An inspired idea you had a couple months back may be the perfect pick when you're panicking the night before your best friend's birthday!

✸ If you see something that absolutely suits someone special in your life but her birthday isn't for six months, buy it anyway and put it in a special box or on a particular shelf that you've set aside just for goods you'll be giving as gifts.

✸ On this gift shelf, keep some items that will suit just about anybody. That way, if someone's birthday sneaks up on you and you don't have time to shop for that one hundred percent perfect gift, you'll still have something really nice to show you care. Neat offerings include: a small photo album or frame, a cool paperback book or CD, a cute pair of hair clips, an inexpensive necklace, a magazine subscription, a pair of movie tickets, or some fancy body lotion.

If nothing you have or can think of seems quite right, remember there are always gift certificates!

Time for Your Family

The people you live with can make your life a pleasure or a real pain. And how you act around 'em can have a major impact on the vibe under your roof. Tend to blow off your little brother? Ignore your dad's questions about how your day was? Though they may bug you in a big way, family members provide you with a great support system that'll last a lifetime.

Before you decide that your parents deserve the award for being the most annoying ones on the block, give some thought as to how things look from where they sit. If you think they are clueless and just don't understand you, maybe that's because whenever they try to get a clue by asking you some questions, you mumble a yes or no answer and then shut yourself in your room. You're the best person to clue them in.

Unless your parents are a total exception to the rule, they want the best for you and they want you to be happy. But you've got to help them out by keeping them informed about your life. Do you really think they'd prefer to see you storming off to your room as you shout, "You just don't understand?" The best way to keep things cool at home is to keep communicating.

Another way to keep the peace on the home front is for you and your family members to have a mutual respect for one another's private time. If you feel like hanging out a big DO NOT DISTURB sign on the doorknob to your room, do it. Just be sure to let people know you don't want to be bugged for a certain amount of time — and then when you're feeling more social, make yourself available.

Usually, when there's conflict in a household it's because the people living under that roof have conflicting priorities. Again, the way to help make life easier for everybody is to let people know what your schedule is like and what's going on with you. They may not realize you need time to yourself to study for an English test if you haven't told 'em that it's on your agenda. If you adhere to the very old but effective adage *Do unto others as you would have them do unto you*, you should be fine when it comes to family matters.

TV or Not TV?

You watch several shows on television every day of the week? Well, you're not alone. Studies show that the average American watches four hours of TV a day! The trick is to not let television take over your life (as in your time, your time here on Earth). Plan to do stuff that's way more of a priority. Hang with your family, volunteer, earn some extra cash, study . . . you get the idea. Watch TV when all those activities have been accomplished. Don't be one of those autopilot hit-the-remote-as-soon-as-I-get-home androids.

You'll find yourself addicted to shows that are beyond stupid. The best technique for taking control of your TV viewing is to sit down with the TV schedule and home in on what's really worth watching. Instead of channel surfing, you'll be channel selecting.

If you find that you're not totally into what you're watching, turn it off. And some shows don't require that you stay stuck to the sofa. You can fix dinner, fold laundry, or tidy up the TV room as you watch and you won't miss a thing. Same goes for those annoying commercial breaks. Look at them as five-minute opportunities to get things done. Unload the dishwasher, get your homework together for the next day, feed the dog.

Don't be held hostage by the time a show airs. Record stuff on the VCR and you can watch it when you want to and fast-forward through all those commercials. Still not convinced that cutting back on the boob tube is really worth it? Consider this: If you cut back on your couch-potato lounge act by five hours a week, you'll have gained yourself eleven days in a year. Not too shabby, wouldn't you say?

Why let some network exec tell you what you must see? Make up your own mind and you'll save yourself hours each week. Say you pick one hour-long show each day. You've just filled up seven hours of your week. Two hours of viewing will gobble up an entire waking day of your week. Take control of that remote and reclaim some hours that are entirely your own. To make a real effort to only watch what you absolutely must see, write your must-see shows down and stick to it!

DAY	SHOW	TIME
Monday		
Tuesday		
Wednesday		
Thursday		
Friday		
Saturday		
Sunday		

Chapter Seven

Fast-forward to Your Future

Get a grip on your time and your space and you're on the road to a future that's big-time bright. Getting into the habit of being organized in terms of school, personal interests, and life at home gears you up for the years ahead when having your act together spells the difference between being average and being awesome. Maybe you haven't thought that far ahead or maybe you feel as if you were born knowing what you want to do for the rest of your life. Either way, it's a great idea to give some thought to your future. While it may seem like you've got years before you're gonna get that high school diploma, it's not too early to check out some of the stuff that'll be out there once you graduate. When you picture your future, remember you are the one holding the paintbrush! Are you doing anything today that'll help you for that tomorrow? Think about it! Ten years from now, if you're stuck in some go-nowhere job, what excuse are you going to offer as to how you ended up in such a position? Wouldn't you rather be able to say that by following a series of steps over a period of time you ended up exactly where you wanted to be?

The Future Is Now

If you've been checking out the stuff in other chapters of this book, you're completely clued in to sticking to schedules, creating calendars, and keeping track of tasks. So put those same principles to work with the Big Picture in mind. Remember . . . you're the artist.

First things first. What would you like to do? Direct movies? Trade on Wall Street? Design software? You're gonna be a whole lot better at something that you actually enjoy. Picture yourself in a certain profession. What time line do you want to draw for yourself?

Put it in writing. As in, "In _____ years, I will be a _____." Now break this big statement into small steps. So you have no idea what your next step would be? Not a big deal. Why not make a trip to the library or log on to a computer? Do some research on your career choice. Keep a file folder full of info you find.

You might discover that certain colleges offer special coursework in what you'll need to study for what you want to do. You may find that there are ways you can volunteer in the field to get a taste of what it would really be like to live the life you're picturing for yourself.

You may want to try to earn some extra money when you realize how many years of study might be required. You could also look into scholarship and financial aid options for the future. Keep at it. Your file folder will expand and your planning and scheduling will begin to take shape. Just as that folder begins to bulge with information, remember you've also added all that new knowledge to your brain.

Chapter Eight
Charts and Lists to Help You Out

This chapter's chock-full of charts and checklists to help you take charge when it comes to Operation Organization. Since this book belongs to you, go ahead and write away. Another option is to use a copier machine to make multiple copies. (You might wanna set the machine on an enlarged setting while you're at it.) Since the idea is for you to make the most of your time and always be adding to your goals, it's a cool idea to have lots of copies to refer to. And since what you've been reading is all about organization, why not create a file folder for 'em, so you'll know where to find 'em?

Brace Yourself for Some Big-time Changes!

Ever wonder where the time goes? Try this. Pick a typical day and log each half hour into this list. You'll be amazed to see where the day takes you and how you can take back some time for yourself! Are you spending much too much time on unimportant things or super-simple tasks? Or do you find large chunks of time that were wasted, spent doing nothing? Once you see what patterns emerge, this is your first step to changing your ways and recapturing lost time. If you discover you tend to waste precious minutes around the same time every day, then maybe you can figure out why and make an effort to focus more during these periods.

	Day:
Time	**Activity**
6:00 A.M.	
6:30 A.M.	
7:00 A.M.	
7:30 A.M.	
8:00 A.M.	
8:30 A.M.	
9:00 A.M.	
9:30 A.M.	
10:00 A.M.	
10:30 A.M.	
11:00 A.M.	
11:30 A.M.	
12:00 P.M.	
12:30 P.M.	
1:00 P.M.	
1:30 P.M.	
2:00 P.M.	
2:30 P.M.	

Time	Day: Activity
3:00 P.M.	
3:30 P.M.	
4:00 P.M.	
4:30 P.M.	
5:00 P.M.	
5:30 P.M.	
6:00 P.M.	
6:30 P.M.	
7:00 P.M.	
7:30 P.M.	
8:00 P.M.	
8:30 P.M.	
9:00 P.M.	
9:30 P.M.	
10:00 P.M.	
10:30 P.M.	
11:00 P.M.	
11:30 P.M.	

Make the Most of Each Month

Odds are there are some things you do each and every month. Could be an ortho appointment, a once-a-month meeting at school, or buying cards for your buds who'll be having a birthday. Whatever it may be, life will be easier if you plug some of those to-dos into position using the chart on the next page. That way, you'll be sure to factor in the time these tasks take and will therefore be better able to budget the rest of your time.

Managing the Month Ahead

Week One

1.
2.
3.
4.
5.

Week Two

1.
2.
3.
4.
5.

Week Three

1.
2.
3.
4.
5.

Week Four

1.
2.
3.
4.
5.

Week Five

1.
2.
3.
4.
5.

A Year to Remember

Take the time to map out five ways you plan to make the most of each month in the upcoming year. Refer back to this list often to keep your priorities straight. These goals can also serve as inspiration when you're feeling overwhelmed — they'll give you something to shoot for.

January

1.
2.
3.
4.
5.

February

1.
2.
3.
4.
5.

March

1.
2.
3.
4.
5.

April

1.
2.
3.
4.
5.

May

1.
2.
3.
4.
5.

June

1.
2.
3.
4.
5.

July

1.
2.
3.
4.
5.

August

1.
2.
3.
4.
5.

September

1.
2.
3.
4.
5.

October

1.
2.
3.
4.
5.

November

1.
2.
3.
4.
5.

December

1.
2.
3.
4.
5.

Chapter Nine

Your *Get It Together* Resource Guide:
Cool Catalogs and Room Redo Resources

Want to write the book on your life? A portable personal organizer could be the answer for you. There are lots of varieties to choose from, and you should be sure to go with a style that is laid out in a way that seems logical and functional to you. While some can leave you feeling as if you've got the whole world in your hands ('cause they include everything you can think of, including foldout maps of the world and charts listing the time zones around the globe), other simpler ones just provide an hourly log so you can keep track of what your day will be about.

Some planners are set up in a way that allows you to plot out the whole month ahead, and others are set up so you can take things one day at a time. Think about the ways you organize your time. If you are more of a look-at-the-big-picture kind of gal, you're likely to prefer something that offers more of an overview. If you're the diva of details, an up-to-the-minute hourly log-in is for you. Some names to look for when you're searching for time-management tools include At-A-Glance, Day Runner, Inc., Day Timer, and Filofax. To check out the different styles, make a trip to an office supply or stationery store.

Study Space and School Supplies

Want to create the perfect study space but feel you need some supplies to create the optimum environment? Here are some companies that offer up awesome accessories for the academic-minded: Avery is all about labels, files, folders, and products that help you get those piles of paperwork under control. Mead is made for study-space organization, too. You can check out the stuff that can help you become totally on the ball by visiting an office supply store.

Room Redo Resources

Want to become an instant interior decorator? Check out the supplies from stores and companies that specialize in organizational accessories.

Rubbermaid

The people at Rubbermaid make tons of products out of plastic. They have bins, buckets, and baskets in dozens of colors that can help you create color-coordinated spots to stash your stuff. Rethink tall kitchen garbage cans; they're perfect for storing tall sports equipment. See-through shoes boxes provide high visibility for little things you want to keep in one place.

Tupperware

Tupperware might make you think of parties your grandma had where she and her friends bought little plastic trays for their deviled eggs. But the Tupperware team has updated their line and come up with some great new organizational tools for rooms and closets, too.

Cool Catalogs

The Container Store

This place has all kinds of goods to help you get organized. While a lot of the stuff is for creating a completely under-control kitchen, you'll also find drawer organizers, stacking shelves and baskets, pull-out stacking basket systems for cupboards and closets, three-tier hanging baskets, and more. For a catalog, call The Container Store at 1-800-733-3532.

Current

The Current catalog offers lots of gifts and gadgets, but you'll also find organizational items such as card organizers for all those birthday cards you've been buying in advance for your buds, an organizer for gift-wrapping paper that can hang in a closet like a garment bag, and folders that allow you to stash away all kinds of stuff. For a catalog, call 1-800-204-2244.

Lillian Vernon

Lillian Vernon catalogs offer lots of gift ideas (many designed for holiday celebrations), but you'll also find wooden file boxes, trunks, blanket racks, an over-the-door canvas CD rack, a cool vinyl magazine rack, in-line skate bags, an over-the-door storage space for small stuffed animals, plus other useful organizational items. Check out the special section of the catalog called Storage Plus! To get a copy of the latest catalog, call 1-800-285-5555.

Hold Everything

Hold Everything's whole reason for existing is organization. Its catalog features products to help organize every room of the house ... and the garage, too! For your room, check out the storage towers, trunks, bedside end tables, CD racks, coat hangers, and hooks. They also carry cool jewelry boxes and cases. For a copy of their catalog, call 1-800-421-2264.

Get Organized!

Right on the cover of this catalog you'll find the words "space-saving innovations to unclutter your life," so you know what it's all about! Room by room is how the organizational products are organized. Go from closet to TV room to bathroom to bedroom to study space for serious solutions to your clutter catastrophes. You can call for a catalog at 1-800-803-9400 or check 'em out on the Web at *www.getorginc.com*

Conclusion

Got It Together?

When you picked up this book, you may have been thinking, *Me, get organized? Yeah, right!* Well, if you decide to put into action even a portion of the pointers you've just read about, you can pretty much count on experiencing a major turnaround — from feeling overwhelmed to feeling much more under control. Just refer back to this book when you need some instant inspiration and remember that the key to getting it together is all about deciding you're gonna be the girl who radiates with an absolute aura of organization!

You'll find that as you become more organized your whole life will begin to run a lot smoother. You won't be as stressed as you head out the door to school, you'll probably find you aren't fighting as often with family members, you'll have more time to hang with your friends, and you're likely to see your grades go up. Even if you opt for only a few of the suggestions in this book, you'll be on your way to making some major changes in how you manage your time and make decisions. Soon you'll be achieving all kinds of personal goals and going places you never dreamed possible. What have you got to lose? Isn't it time to say good-bye to clutter, confusion, chaos, and conflict? Introduce yourself to organization and you'll be on your way to getting together everything in your life!